Brahms Masterpieces
for Solo Piano
38 Works

JOHANNES BRAHMS

Edited by
Eusebius Mandyczewski
for the Vienna Gesellschaft der Musikfreunde Edition

DOVER PUBLICATIONS, INC.
Mineola, New York

Bibliographical Note

This Dover edition, first published in 1998, is a new compilation of thirty-eight works from Vols. 13, 14 and 15 of *Johannes Brahms, Sämtliche Werke / Ausgabe der Gesellschaft der Musikfreunde in Wien*, originally published by Breitkopf & Härtel, Leipzig, n.d. [1926–7]. New main headings have been added throughout.

International Standard Book Number: 0-486-40149-9

Manufactured in the United States of America
Dover Publications, Inc., 31 East 2nd Street, Mineola, N.Y. 11501

CONTENTS

Ballade in D Minor

No. 1 of *Four Ballades*, Op. 10 (1854)

From the Scottish ballad "Edward"
in Johann Gottfried von Herder's folksong collection *Stimmen der Völker*

Capriccio in B Minor

No. 2 of *Eight Piano Pieces*, Op. 76 (1878)

Capriccio in G Minor

No. 3 of [7] *Fantasies*, Op. 116 (1892)

Hungarian Dances

Seven of twenty-one Hungarian Dances originally composed
for piano four hands (1852–69); solo arrangements by the composer (1872)

1

2

Allegro non assai

3

4

5

6

Allegretto vivace

7

Intermezzo in B-flat Major

No. 4 of *Eight Piano Pieces*, Op. 76 (1878)

Intermezzo in A Minor

No. 2 of [7] *Fantasies*, Op. 116 (1892)

Intermezzo in B-flat Minor

No. 2 of *Three Intermezzos*, Op. 117 (1892)

Andante non troppo e con molto espressione

Intermezzo in C-sharp Minor

No. 3 of *Three Intermezzos*, Op. 117 (1892)

Intermezzo in A Major

No. 2 of [6] *Piano Pieces*, Op. 118 (1892)

Intermezzo in E-flat Minor

No. 6 of [6] *Piano Pieces*, Op. 118 (1892)

Dedicated to Elisabeth von Herzogenberg

Rhapsody in B Minor

No. 1 of *Two Rhapsodies*, Op. 79 (1879)

1

in tempo

Rhapsody in G Minor

No. 2 of *Two Rhapsodies*, Op. 79 (1879)

Molto passionato, ma non troppo allegro.

Rhapsody in E-flat Major

No. 4 of [4] *Piano Pieces*, Op. 119 (1892)

Allegro risoluto

Waltzes

[16] *Waltzes*, Op. 39, originally composed for piano four hands (1865);
simplified solo arrangements by the composer

Sonata No. 3 in F Minor

Op. 5 (1853)

*) Die kleinen Noten können nötigenfalls wegbleiben.

* The smaller notes may be omitted if necessary.

Andante

Der Abend dämmert, das Mondlicht scheint,
Da sind zwei Herzen in Liebe vereint
Und halten sich selig umfangen.

Sternau

Andante espressivo

ben cantando

a tempo

Scherzo

Dal segno sino al Fine.

Intermezzo

Rückblick [*Backward Glance*]

Finale

Allegro moderato ma rubato

Variations and Fugue
on a Theme by Handel
Op. 24 (1861)

Var. 14

Var. 21

Var. 25

Fuga

Variations
on a Theme by Paganini
Op. 35 (1862–3)

FIRST SET

Thema
Non troppo presto

Var. 1

Var. 10

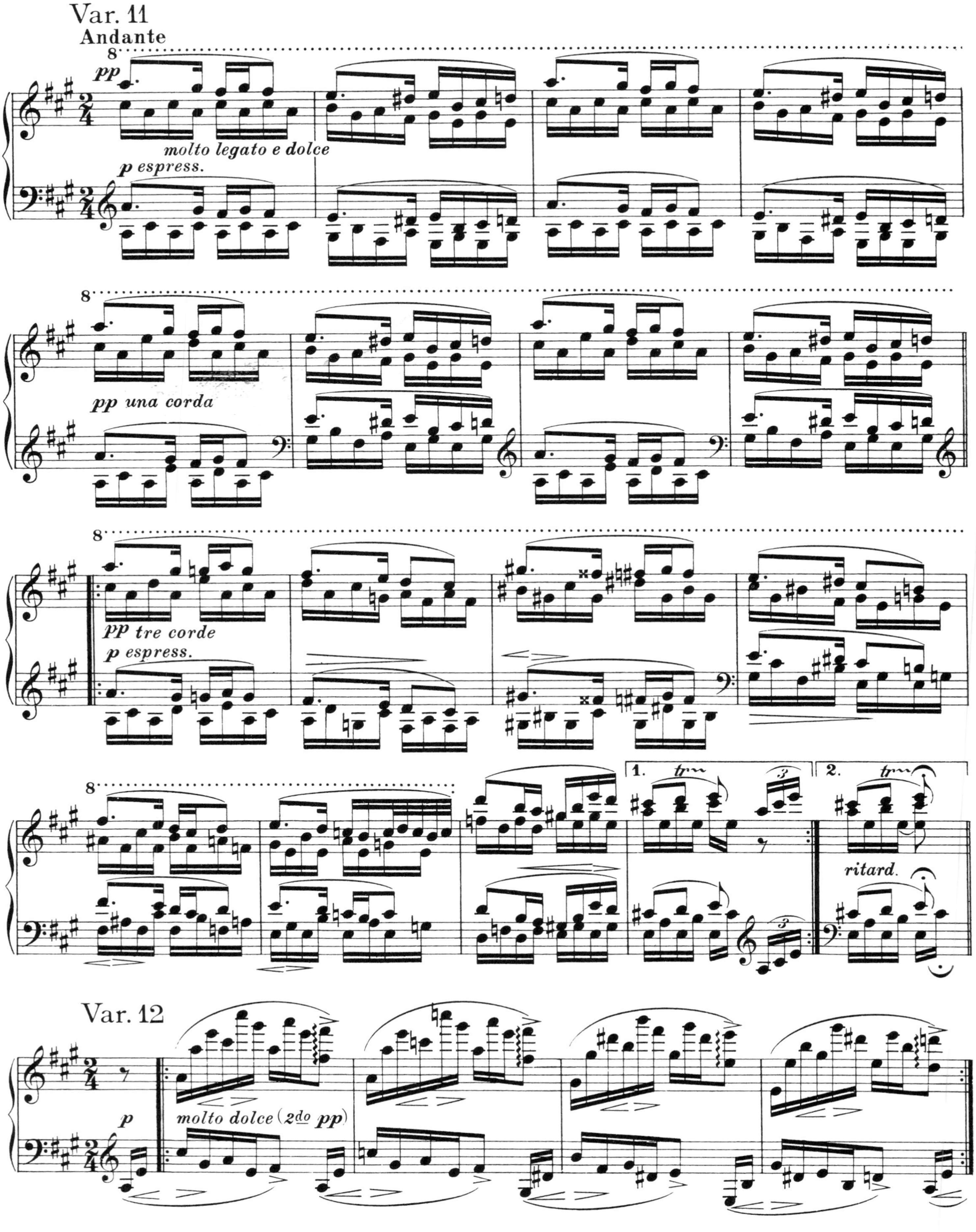
Var. 11
Andante
pp
molto legato e dolce
p espress.
pp una corda
pp tre corde
p espress.
1.
2.
ritard.
Var. 12
p
molto dolce (2do pp)

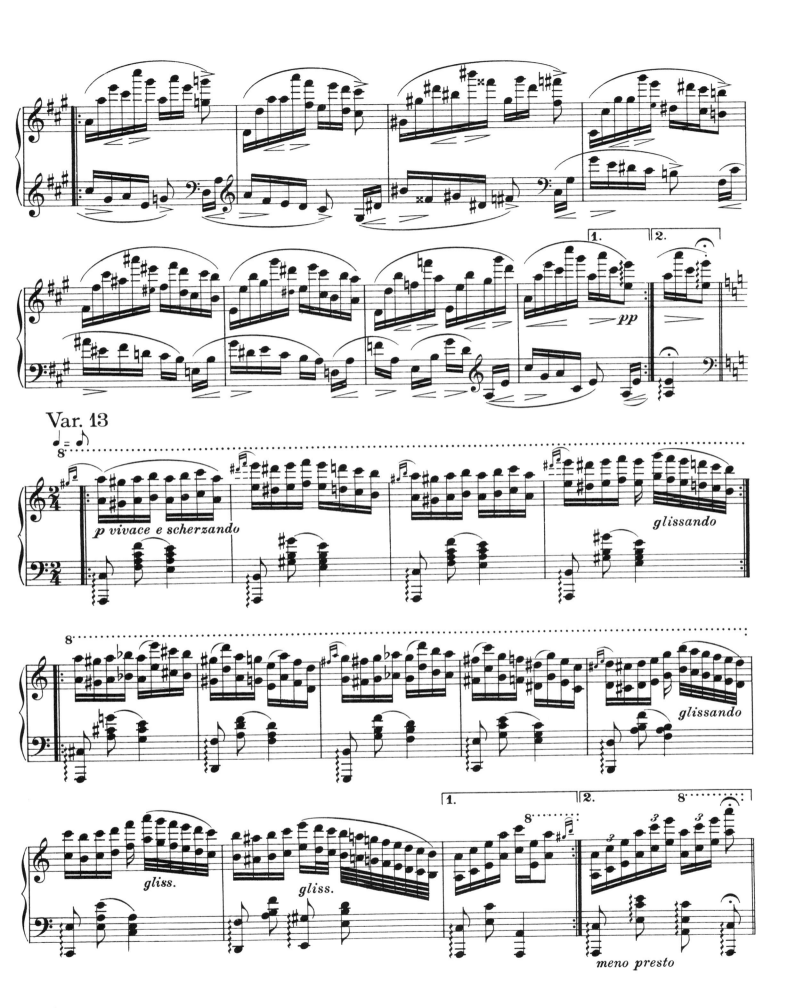

Var. 13

Var. 14
Allegro

Thema
Non troppo presto

Var. 2
Poco animato

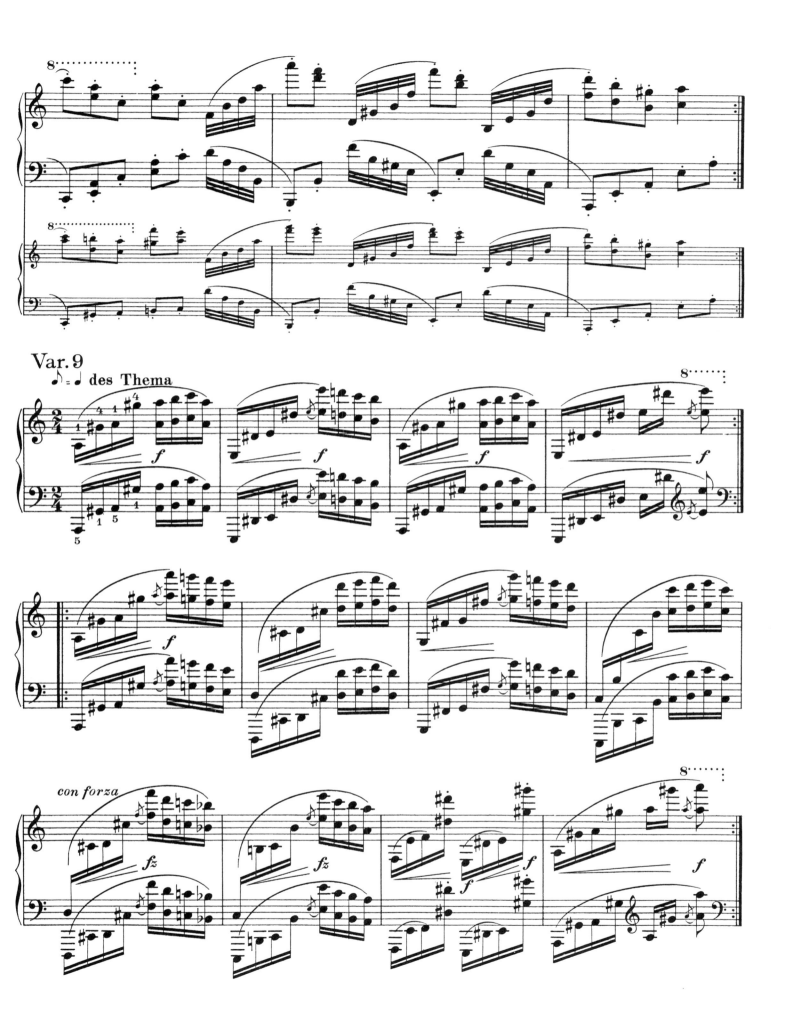

Var. 10
Feroce, energico

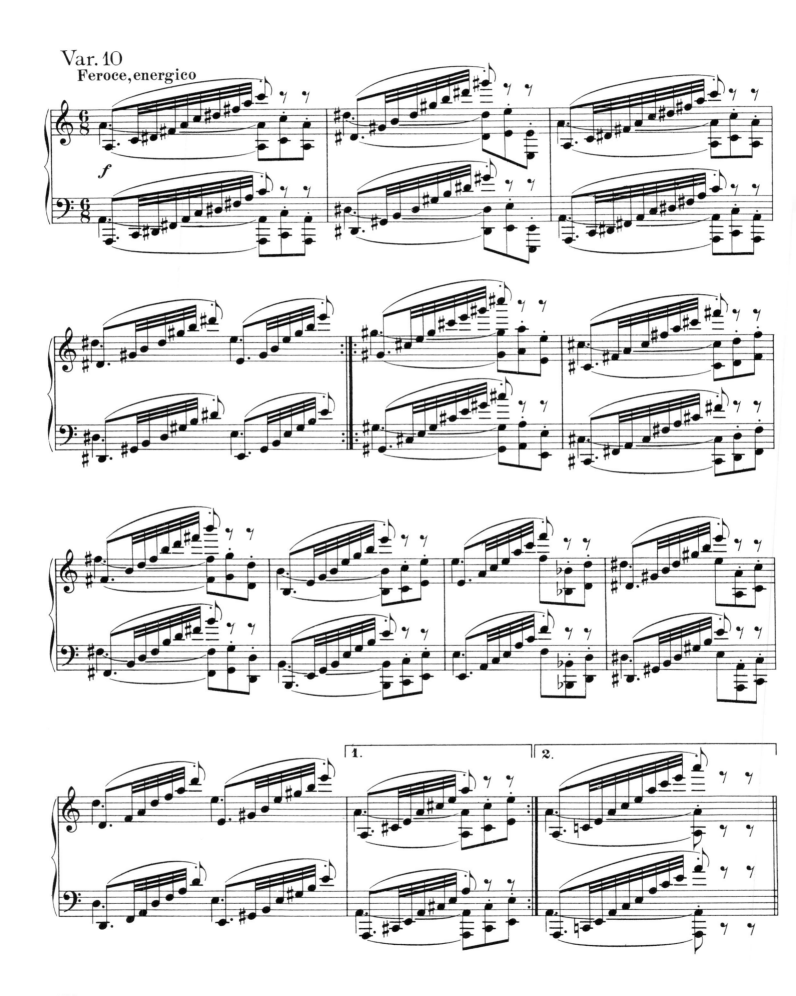

Var. 13
Un poco più Andante

END OF EDITION